"Chambers helped me learn how to work in front of the camera. Before I met him, I was shy. Now, I'm starring in a TV show!"

—DEE DEE DAVIS, ACTRESS
THE BERNIE MAC SHOW

"His knowledge of the craft of acting, coupled with his passionate love for the art, makes Chambers simply one of the best acting coaches in Los Angeles...or anywhere else. When I'm casting, I can always spot Chambers' students. His material is unique, and the young actors are head-and-shoulders above the rest."

—ANDY FICKMAN
WRITER/DIRECTOR

"I have known Chambers Stevens for almost twenty years and it doesn't surprise me in the least that his ability to zoom in on bull's eye monologues and scenes for today's youth is accurate and tasteful. As a veteran theatre arts secondary teacher of three decades, I can shout from the housetops how frustrating it is to match scenes, young actors, and interest level in a happy and comfortable marriage of talent. I have spent countless hours at Drama Bookshop on Times Square searching for appropriate audition material. Finally, the search is over!"

—KENT CATHCART, LEAD TEACHER, SPEECH AND DRAMA
McGAVOCK HIGH SCHOOL
NASHVILLE, TN

"His energy and enthusiasm are contagious. He makes you want to perform. Chambers makes you believe you can do it."

—RHONDA GAMBREL, COMMUNITY RELATIONS MANAGER
BARNES & NOBLE BOOKSELLERS
WILLOW GROVE, PA

"I've seen students transform under Chambers' guidance. He inspires them to do their best."

—APRIL MARTIN, *WEST VIRGINIA STATE COLLEGE, WV*

Sensational Scenes for Kids
Copyright © 2004 by Chambers Stevens

What Others Are Saying About the Hollywood 101 series

Hollywood 101's *Magnificent Monologues for Kids* "will fill a gap in library collections, whether as a source for auditioning materials or for short oral presentations."

—BOOKLIST, AMERICAN LIBRARY ASSOCIATION

"Chambers Stevens' event was fun and refreshing. One of the best events we've ever hosted. {He} helped build self-confidence in girls, brought out their personalities, even the shyest ones participated. And the miracle was that boys were attending and participating. It was great to see. A very hip event!"

—LEIGH MACARIO, COMMUNITY RELATIONS COORDINATOR
BORDERS BOOKS & MUSIC
WESTBURY, NY

"Chambers makes you learn and laugh at the same time!"

—LARA TELLIS, STUDENT
GEORGE WASHINGTON HIGH SCHOOL

"Like the other entries in this series, this volume {Sensational Scenes for Teens} offers young actors fresh audition material written by an acting coach who works with kids...The contemporary urban and suburban settings coupled with culturally neutral names allow for racial and ethnic diversity. Libraries that serve growing drama programs would certainly want to consider purchasing this title."

—SCHOOL LIBRARY JOURNAL

"Chambers is a great actor. Always creative and convincing and totally honest."

—CARRIE SMITH, STUDENT, DUNBAR, WV

Hollywood 101

SENSATIONAL SCENES for kids

"The Scene Study-guide for Young Actors!"

by

Chambers Stevens

SANDCASTLE
PUBLISHING &
DISTRIBUTION
south pasadena, california

Sensational Scenes for Kids: The Scene Study-guide for Young Actors!
Copyright © 2004 by Chambers Stevens
Book Cover & Interior Design by Renee Rolle-Whatley
Book Cover Photography by Nathan Hope
The images used herein were obtained from IMSI's Master Clips©/MasterPhotos© Collection, 1895
Francisco Blvd. East, San Rafael, CA 94901-5506, USA

Actors in Cover Photograph: Back: Jazmin Williams, Stephen Markarian, Chelsea Larner, Ricky Butler; Middle:
Christian Lavery, Katie MaKain, Calob Lostutter, Dana Benedict; Bottom Row: Adam Gabriel, Jasmine Black

Published by: Sandcastle Publishing & Distribution

Post Office Box 3070
South Pasadena, CA 91031-6070
Phone/Website (800) 891-4204, www.childrenactingbooks.com

Publisher's Cataloging in Publication
(Provided by Quality Books, Inc.)

Stevens, Chambers.
    Sensational scenes for kids : "the scene study-guide
for young actors!" / Chambers Stevens,
    p. cm. -- (Hollywood 101 ; 5)
    Includes bibliographical references and index.
    SUMMARY: Collection of original comedic and dramatic
scenes for young actors in various numbers and
combinations.
    Audience: Grades 1-7.
    ISBN: 1-883995-12-4

    1. Acting--Juvenile literature. 2. Teenagers--Drama
--Juvenile literature. [1. Acting.] 3. Acting--Auditions
I. Title. II. Series.

PN2080.S74 2002   792'.02
                                   QBI03-700509

First Printing 9/2003

Printed and bound in China
10 09 08 07 06   12 11 10 9 8 7 6 5 4 3 2

Table of Contents

Dedication

TO
ANGELA WIBKING-FOX

YOUR BELIEF IN ME
HELPED ME ACHIEVE SO MANY OF MY GOALS.
FOR THAT, I AM VERY GRATEFUL.

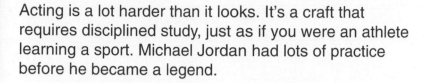

Acting is a lot harder than it looks. It's a craft that requires disciplined study, just as if you were an athlete learning a sport. Michael Jordan had lots of practice before he became a legend.

To become a great actor, you have to know how to play a scene. Once you've grasped scene study, you will not only audition well but also have the necessary skills to act a role. We all remember the moment Frodo was given the ring. Imagine if his reaction had been nonchalance and the actor, in this case Elijah Wood, decided to juggle the ring and casually throw it in his pocket. It wouldn't make sense. When Juni in <u>Spy Kids</u> ran after Carmen, imagine if the actor had slowed his movement down and lethargically said his lines. These are obvious acting choices to avoid, but for every simple choice, there are many difficult ones.

Please notice my use of the words choice and decision in the last paragraph. While there are certain rules to acting, there are numerous ways to approach a moment. At the end of the day, *you*, the actor, will have to decide. Think of it in reference to basketball again. Michael Jordan can use different shots to make a basket, but the end goal of a sunk basket is always the same.

To nail a moment, our equivalent of scoring, you must understand the basics. This book will teach you about structure, character, and personal perspective (yours,

 **Foreword**

that is) while you prepare scenes. Remember some of your favorite lines from movies, maybe lines like *"Me Tarzan, you Jane," "May the Force be with you,"* and *"E.T. phone home."* You hear the line and how it was said. These acting choices had everything to do with the story, the character, and the actor's own personality. As a result, a memorable and likable character was created. These actors did, however, have some help and that's where a coach comes into play.

Chamber Stevens is one of the best coaches you will find as a young actor. He's one of the most in-demand teachers in Hollywood because his lessons are accessible and applicable. His extensive work in multiple areas of entertainment as a director, writer, and actor, gives him a dialogue with his students that allows them to produce results. He makes it easy to understand how to act.

So, my invitation is to turn the page and see for yourself. If you've gotten this far, you've definitely entered the game. Congratulations and good luck.

—KRISTIN CASKEY
2-TIME TONY AWARD-WINNING PRODUCER

Kristin Caskey's first acting role (<u>Mother Goose Goes to Hollywood</u>) and her last acting role (<u>Vivisections from the Blown Mind</u>) were both as a producer. She believes it was an omen. Ms. Caskey is a 2-time Tony Award-winning producer of such Broadway productions as <u>Thoroughly Modern Millie</u>, <u>One Flew Over the Cuckoo's Nest,</u> and <u>You're A Good Man, Charlie Brown</u>. She is the Vice-President of Fox Theatricals and lives in New York City with her husband, Tom.

Introduction

For over a decade, I've been an acting coach in Los Angeles. The kids I've coached have worked on Broadway, in major motion pictures and in television: on ABC, NBC, CBS, FOX, WB, The Disney Channel, and Nickelodeon. They've also done voice-overs for cartoons and video games, series on the internet, and countless commercials.

How do these kids get all these jobs? Well, I would like to think that it's because they have a great coach. But the truth is—they practice. While many kids in America are playing video games, practicing soccer, or doing their homework, many young actors are practicing their craft of acting. They take classes, learn lines, and go to auditions. If you want to do well in sports, you have to go to practice. It's the same for acting. I hope this book will help you exercise your talent.

In **SENSATIONAL SCENES FOR KIDS: THE SCENE STUDY-GUIDE FOR YOUNG ACTORS!** you will find scenes that could be on today's TV shows. Some are funny; some are serious. I've also included a number of exercises you can work on while performing the scenes. Be sure to check the pages near the end of the book—you know, the glossary— where you will find words every professional actor should know. Lastly, I've included a guide to my favorite movies starring kids. You can learn something from every one of these performances.

Break-a-leg. And most importantly, have fun.

Scene Styles

Let's start with an important lesson. There are two different types of scene structures presented in this book:

- Half-hour comedies

- One-hour dramas/film scripts

Half-hour comedy scripts like *Sabrina, the Teenage Witch* and *Lizzy McQuire* look like this:

<u>INT. THE SCIENCE LAB</u>

HOWIE IS WORKING ON A SCIENCE EXPERIMENT WHEN DANNY ENTERS.

                    DANNY
          Hey Howie! How's it going?

                    HOWIE
          Danny, I haven't seen you in a while.

Notice that the stage direction, the line that starts HOWIE IS—, is typed in capital letters. Also notice that the slugline, that's the line that tells us where the scene takes place, is underlined. By the way, INT. stands for interior and means inside. EXT. stands for Exterior and means outside.

One-hour drama scripts like *7th Heaven*, and film scripts like *Spy Kids* look like this:

INT. AN OLD DESERTED HOUSE

Sam, Lane, and Martin enter.

SAM
This is freaky.

LANE
You're telling me.

MARTIN
Guys, maybe we shouldn't be in here.

Notice the slugline is not underlined. Also, the stage directions are in lower and uppercase letters.

Okay, you say. I understand the difference. Now, what good does it do me? Well, plenty.

Half-hour comedy shows are taped before a live audience. An actor performing in a half-hour show must understand that, as in a play, he/she must hold for laughs. There are usually four cameras and the actors rehearse for a couple of days before taping. The actual taping usually lasts about four hours.

Hour-long shows and movies are filmed with one camera. There is no audience and usually no rehearsal. Filming an hour drama can take as long as 7 to 8 days. Filming a movie can takes months.

There are of course exceptions, but in Hollywood, that's usually the case.

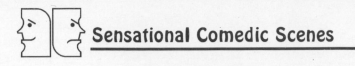
Sensational Comedic Scenes for Kids!

The Scene Study-guide for Young Actors!
Copyright © 2004 by Chambers Stevens

Tom

INT. BILLY'S ROOM

BILLY ENTERS. HE PUTS DOWN HIS SCHOOL BOOKS AND THEN
SITS ON THE BED TO UNTIE HIS SHOES. BUT THERE IS ALREADY
SOMEONE SITTING ON HIS BED, ALSO UNTYING HIS SHOES.

                    BILLY
          Ahhh!

                    ANOTHER BILLY
          Ahhh!!!

                    BILLY
          What are you doing in my room?

                    ANOTHER BILLY
          This is my room.

                    BILLY
          How did you get in here?

                    ANOTHER BILLY
          I have a key. Are you a robber or something?

                    BILLY
          This is my room! Look, you better get
          out before I call the police.

                    ANOTHER BILLY
          You better get out before I call the police.

                    BILLY
          (Picking up his baseball bat) I'm warning you.

                    ANOTHER BILLY
          What are you some kind of maniac or something?

                    BILLY
          This is my room. This is my house. This is my bed.
          See that sign above the bed? It says, "Billy's room."

                    ANOTHER BILLY
          And that's me. I'm Billy!

BILLY

No, I'm Billy!

ANOTHER BILLY

Oh no. It happened again. Shoot.

BILLY

What are you talking about?

ANOTHER BILLY

Somehow we mixed up universes.

BILLY

What?

ANOTHER BILLY

It's really complicated. But basically, your name
is Billy Ferris, right?

BILLY

Yeah.

ANOTHER BILLY

Well, my name is Billy Ferris too. And I bet you
like baseball, tacos, and video games.

BILLY

Yeah. But that's easy to guess. Look around my room.
I'm holding a baseball bat. There's a taco wrapper on the
floor. And my video game system is hooked up to my TV.

ANOTHER BILLY

Okay well how about this. I know you
have a crush on Erin Knapp.

BILLY

(Shocked) How did you know that? I
haven't told anyone about Erin.

ANOTHER BILLY

Because I have a crush on Erin Knapp too! See we are
the same person except in different universes.

BILLY

But we look nothing alike.

Sensational Comedic Scenes: (Two Kids)

ANOTHER BILLY

That's cause I'm the good-looking Billy in the good-looking universe.

BILLY

And what am I?

ANOTHER BILLY

You're the average Billy in the average universe.

BILLY

I think you've got that mixed up. I'm better looking than you.

ANOTHER BILLY

You really think so?

BILLY

Yeah.

ANOTHER BILLY

Then I was wrong. You are the stupid Billy in the stupid universe. Well, I've got to go. Erin and I have a date.

BILLY

What? You asked her out?

ANOTHER BILLY

Yeah. She's a real cutie.

BILLY

But I like her.

ANOTHER BILLY

But you're too stupid to do anything about it. See you around Billy.

ANOTHER BILLY EXITS.

BILLY

Maybe I am the stupid Billy in the stupid universe.

Arrested

<u>EXT. IN FRONT OF THE SCHOOL</u>

MALCOLM IS LEAVING SCHOOL WHEN HE ACCIDENTALLY DROPS HIS PAPERS.

> MALCOLM

Shoot.

MALCOLM BENDS DOWN TO GET HIS PAPERS WHEN KENNY RUNS ON.

> KENNY

Hold it right there. You're under arrest.

> MALCOLM

What?

> KENNY

Don't move or I'll have to call for backup.

> MALCOLM

What are you talking about?

> KENNY

You, my friend, are under arrest for littering school property. Now give me your name before I also charge you with resisting arrest.

> MALCOLM

I didn't litter! I just dropped these papers.

> KENNY

Yeah? Tell that to the judge. (Pulling out his ticket book) Now what is your name?

> MALCOLM

Malcolm Harper. Hey, why are you writing all this down?

> KENNY

To put on your record. Now you have the right to remain silent...

MALCOLM

Wait, you can't arrest me. You're just a kid.

KENNY

A kid who is making a citizen's
arrest.

MALCOLM

A what?

KENNY

That's what you do if you're not a policeman. Now where
was I? Shoot, now you've made me lose my place. Okay,
I'm starting back at the beginning. You have the right to
remain silent...

MALCOLM

Hold it! You can't arrest me. I'm arresting you.

KENNY

For what?

MALCOLM

(Trying to think of something) For...uh...not tucking in
your shirt on school property.

KENNY

That's not a law.

MALCOLM

Tell that to the judge. Now what is your name?

KENNY

Kenny Michaels.

MALCOLM

Well, Kenny you have the right to remain silent....

KENNY

(Falling on his knees) Wait! Please don't take me to jail. I
can't be locked up. It will embarrass my family and ruin my
grades. And I'll lose weight 'cause jail food is really
horrible. Please, please don't arrest me.

> MALCOLM

Okay. But stand up and tuck in your shirt

> KENNY

(Standing up) Thank you, thank you.

> MALCOLM

Just don't let it happen again. Now get out of here before I think of another reason to arrest you.

> KENNY

Yes, sir. Thank you, sir.

KENNY RUNS OFF.

> MALCOLM

That kid needs help.

Best Friends

<u>INT. THE LUNCH ROOM</u>

BRENDA IS SITTING IN THE LUNCH ROOM BY HERSELF WHEN
DWIGHT WALKS UP WITH HIS LUNCH TRAY.

> **DWIGHT**
> Can I sit down?

> **BRENDA**
> (Looking at him with disgust) Whatever.

DWIGHT SITS DOWN.

> **DWIGHT**
> (Looking at his food) This food is so gross. Does this even
> look like a taco to you?

> **BRENDA**
> Don't blame me if you're too stupid to bring your lunch.

> **DWIGHT**
> It's my first day at school. I just moved here on Monday.

> **BRENDA**
> Did your last school have good food?

> **DWIGHT**
> No.

> **BRENDA**
> Then you're stupid for thinking this one would.

> **DWIGHT**
> What is your problem?

> **BRENDA**
> My problem is I was trying to read before you came along
> and started showing me your gross food.

DWIGHT
I see now why you were sitting alone. You have a bad attitude.

BRENDA
(Getting angry) I sit alone because I hate everyone at this school. Including the new students.

DWIGHT
Girl, you are whacked.

BRENDA
(Jumping up) THEN GET AWAY FROM MY TABLE!!!

DWIGHT
(Softly) No.

BRENDA
GET OUT OF HERE!!

DWIGHT
(Still softly) No!

BRENDA SLAMS HER BOOK ON THE TABLE AS SHE SITS DOWN. A BEAT.

DWIGHT (cont'd)
So let me guess, everyone picks on you.

BRENDA
If you are going to sit here then shut up.

DWIGHT
People picked on me at my old school. Guys would beat me up. Girls would laugh at me.

BRENDA
It's because you're stupid.

DWIGHT
Maybe. But I like to think it's because they're stupid.

BRENDA LOOKS AT HIM A SECOND.

BRENDA

(Laughing) They are.

DWIGHT

You have a nice smile.

BRENDA

Shut up.

DWIGHT

You do.

BRENDA

Whatever.

DWIGHT

Look, since this in my first day I could use a friend.

BRENDA

Don't look at me.

DWIGHT

Why not?

BRENDA

'Cause I don't like to have friends. They're always buggin' you all the time. Ask you to go places with them.

DWIGHT

(Laughing) Yeah, it's a real bummer when people like you.

BRENDA

(Laughing) Shut up.

DWIGHT

Sorry, I can't. I don't listen to anyone who's not my friend.

BRENDA

If I was your friend would you shut up?

DWIGHT

Yep.

BRENDA

Okay then, we're friends.

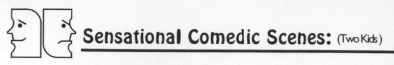

> DWIGHT

Cool.

> BRENDA

(Laughing) Now shut up.

> DWIGHT

(Laughing) Is that any way to treat your best friend?

> BRENDA

You're not my best friend.

> DWIGHT

Do you have any other friends?

> BRENDA

No.

> DWIGHT

Then I'm your best.

The Cookie

INT. CHRIS' ROOM

CHRIS IS DOING HIS HOMEWORK WHEN MAGGIE WALKS IN
EATING A COOKIE.

> MAGGIE
> (Teasing him) Yum. This is so good.

> CHRIS
> Hey, I want a cookie.

> MAGGIE
> Sorry but this is the last one. (Taking a big bite) Ummmmmmm.
> Don't you just love chocolate?

> CHRIS
> Wait a minute. Mom bought a whole package of chocolate chip
> cookies yesterday.

> MAGGIE
> I know. They were so good.

> CHRIS
> You ate the whole package?

> MAGGIE
> There's some crumbs left.

> CHRIS
> That's all? They're all gone?

> MAGGIE
> (Teasing him) All gone.

> CHRIS
> Yes!!! (Yelling offstage) Mom, you owe me ten dollars!!! Yes!!!

> MAGGIE
> What are you talking about?

> CHRIS
> I bet Mom ten bucks you would eat all of the cookies.

> MAGGIE
> You didn't.

> CHRIS
> Did. I thought it would at least take you a week. But you ate
> them in twenty-four hours. Yes! (Yelling offstage) Mom, pay up!!!

Sensational Comedic Scenes: (Two Kids)

> **MAGGIE**
> Wait. Look. I still have one bite left.

> **CHRIS**
> So?

> **MAGGIE**
> So, I didn't eat all of the cookies. You get nothing.
> (Yelling offstage) Mom, guess what?!!!

> **CHRIS**
> Wait! Wait! I'll make you a deal. Eat that last bite and
> I'll give you a dollar.

> **MAGGIE**
> (Yelling offstage) Mom!

CHRIS JUMPS UP AND PUTS HIS HAND OVER MAGGIE'S MOUTH.

> **CHRIS**
> Okay. Two dollars.

MAGGIE SHAKES HER HEAD NO.

> **CHRIS (cont'd)**
> Half. I'll give you half. Five dollars.

MAGGIE DOESN'T MOVE. SO CHRIS SLOWLY TAKES HIS HAND OFF
HER MOUTH.

> **MAGGIE**
> Five dollars and fifty cents.

> **CHRIS**
> No way.

> **MAGGIE**
> (Yelling offstage) Mom!!!

> **CHRIS**
> Okay. Okay. Five fifty.

> **MAGGIE**
> (Holding her hand out) Deal.

> **CHRIS**
> (Shaking her hand) Deal.

The Scene Study-guide for Young Actors!
Copyright © 2004 by Chambers Stevens

> **MAGGIE**
> I guess that'll teach you to bet against me.

> **CHRIS**
> Yep. Looks like you are too smart for me. So can I have that last bite of cookie?

> **MAGGIE**
> Sure.

SHE HOLDS OUT THE LAST BITE OF COOKIE. CHRIS REACHES FOR IT. BUT AT THE LAST SECOND, MAGGIE POPS IT INTO HER MOUTH.

> **MAGGIE (cont'd)**
> Sucker!

CHRIS STARES AT HER A BEAT.

> **CHRIS**
> Mom! You owe me ten bucks!!!!

> **MAGGIE**
> Oh, no.

Dance

<u>INT. A DANCE STUDIO</u>

KAREN, THE BALLERINA, IS STRETCHING WHEN PEACHES ENTERS.
KAREN IS IN A BLACK LEOTARD AND PEACHES IS IN BRIGHT COL-
ORED DANCE CLOTHES.

> PEACHES
> Wow, you can really stretch!

KAREN IGNORES HER.

> PEACHES (cont'd)
> This is the jazz dance class isn't it?

> KAREN
> (Turning away) Yes.

> PEACHES
> Oh good! Man, you really are in good shape.

> KAREN
> Excuse me, I don't really like to talk before class.

> PEACHES
> Why?

> KAREN
> Because I need to mentally prepare.

> PEACHES
> (Laughing) That is the stupidest thing I've ever heard.

> KAREN
> I don't care what you think.

> PEACHES
> I'm sorry, I didn't mean to insult you.

> KAREN
> You didn't. To be insulted you have to care what someone says.
> And I could care less about anything you say.

> PEACHES
> That was mean.

> KAREN
> Please stop talking!!!

PEACHES
Look we got off to a bad start. (Trying to shake her hand)
My name is Peaches.

KAREN
(Turning away) I don't care.

PEACHES
You will.

THE MUSIC COMES ON AND PEACHES AND KAREN START TO
DANCE. PEACHES IS A MUCH BETTER DANCER THAN KAREN. THE
DANCE GETS WILDER AND KAREN FALLS DOWN. THE MUSIC
STOPS.

KAREN
Ow! I think I sprained my ankle.

PEACHES
Let me see.

PEACHES PICKS UP KAREN'S ANKLE.

KAREN
Ooooooooooooow!!!!!!

PEACHES
Yep, it's sprained.

KAREN
Will you help me up? I need to go see the nurse.

PEACHES
Oh, so now you need me?

KAREN
I'm hurt.

PEACHES
You mean like I was when you wouldn't talk to me?

KAREN
You've got a point. I'm sorry.

PEACHES
That's better. (Helping her up) Now lean on me.

KAREN
Thanks for helping me, Peaches.

PEACHES
I told you you'd need to know my name.

Excuses

INT. THE GIRL'S BATHROOM

LEE IS PUTTING ON LIP GLOSS WHEN BONNIE ENTERS CARRYING
HER SCHOOL BOOKS.

> **BONNIE**
> There you are. I've been looking all over for you.

> **LEE**
> Really? I've been in here.

> **BONNIE**
> Well, you were supposed to help me put up the Halloween class
> decorations.

> **LEE**
> Oh...well...I couldn't because...

> **BONNIE**
> Excuses, excuses, Lee all you ever do is make excuses.

> **LEE**
> That's not true.

> **BONNIE**
> It is. Take today. You were supposed to turn in your science
> project and you told Mrs. Rainer that your pet snake ate it.

> **LEE**
> Slimey did eat it. If you don't believe me you can call the vet.

> **BONNIE**
> What about last week when you told me that you couldn't come
> over and help me bake cookies 'cause you had to have
> your leg amputated?

> **LEE**
> That was true, too!

> **BONNIE**
> But you have two legs. So how did you have one cut off?

> **LEE**
> (Laughing) Didn't I tell you?

> **BONNIE**
> No.

> **LEE**
> Well...when I got to the hospital the doctor told me that they
> found a cure to my disease. So my leg is healed.

BONNIE
(Not believing her) They found a cure?

LEE
Yep! Lip gloss. (Holding up her lip gloss) This is a special medicated lip gloss.

BONNIE
This is silly. I can't believe this.

LEE
It's true.

BONNIE
Fine, whatever. But why didn't you help me with the Halloween decorations?

LEE
Oh...well, I...

BONNIE
Now don't make up an excuse. Tell me the truth.

LEE
Okay. The truth is I couldn't help you because I'm allergic to orange.

BONNIE
Oranges?

LEE
No, not the fruit. Orange. The color.

BONNIE
Give me a break.

LEE
You don't believe me? It's true. Every time I get near orange I break out and start having attacks.

BONNIE
Really? Well I just happen to have a piece of orange paper with me.

BONNIE PULLS OUT A PIECE OF ORANGE PAPER. LEE STARES AT IT FOR A SECOND.

LEE
Oh my gosh, I'm cured! I can't believe it.

BONNIE
You're not the only one.

Family Love

<u>INT. THE FAMILY ROOM</u>

SOPHIE AND SAMMY ARE SITTING ON THE COUCH WITH THEIR
ARMS AROUND EACH OTHER. THEY ARE BROTHER AND SISTER.

> SAMMY
> This is stupid.

> SOPHIE
> Don't talk to me. Your breath stinks.

SAMMY BREATHES ON HER.

> SOPHIE (cont'd)
> Gross! What have you been eating?!!!

> SAMMY
> Beef jerky. Teriyaki flavored.

SAMMY BREATHS ON HER AGAIN.

> SOPHIE
> (Yelling) MOM!

SAMMY PUTS HIS HANDS ON HER MOUTH.

> SAMMY
> Shut up! If Mom comes in here she'll make us sit like this forever.

SAMMY SLOWLY TAKES HIS HANDS OFF HER MOUTH.

> SOPHIE
> Well, if you would leave me alone we wouldn't always get in trouble.

> SAMMY
> I'm not the one always yelling for Mom!

> SOPHIE
> Whatever.

> SAMMY
> (Mimics her) "Whatever."

SOPHIE
Stop it!

SAMMY
(Mimicking her again.) "Stop it!"

SOPHIE
(Threatening her) Do you want me to call Mom?

SAMMY
Go ahead. She'll be mad at you, too.

SOPHIE
I hate this. Where did she get this idea anyway?

SAMMY
(Reaching over to the coffee table and grabbing a book) This!

SOPHIE
(Reading the cover) "What to do if your kids hate each other."

SAMMY
That's us.

SOPHIE
Yeah.

SAMMY
(Opening book) "One of the best things to do is force them
to be together. Next time they have a fight make them
sit on the couch and hold each other. You will see a bond
forming in no time."

SOPHIE
That's stupid.

SAMMY
Yeah.

SOPHIE
Who wrote that book anyway?

SAMMY
Probably someone who never had a brother or a sister.

SOPHIE
Yeah. Wouldn't it be great to be an only child?

SAMMY
I'd love it.

SOPHIE
No you wouldn't. 'Cause you wouldn't have me to pick on.

SAMMY
(Laughing) And you wouldn't have me to tell on.

SOPHIE
(Starts laughing) I'd miss that. Can you scratch my shoulder?

SAMMY DOES.

SOPHIE (cont'd)
Ah that feels good.

SAMMY KEEPS SCRATCHING. AFTER A BEAT HE STOPS.

SOPHIE (cont'd)
Thanks.

SAMMY
Does my breath really stink?

SOPHIE
Nah. I was just picking on you.

SAMMY
(Laughing) I believed you.

SOPHIE
I'm not as stupid as you think I am.

SAMMY
Course not. You're related to me.

Fast

EXT. THE FOOTBALL FIELD

STEVE COMES RUNNING ON THE FIELD. TEN SECONDS LATER
CLINT RUNS UP BEHIND HIM.

> CLINT
> (Out of breath) Man, you are fast! I had no idea you could
> run like that.

> STEVE
> You think so?

> CLINT
> Are you crazy? You've got to be the fastest kid in the school.
> Wait till the coach sees you.

> STEVE
> Thanks, Clint, for helping me get ready for tryouts.

> CLINT
> Sure thing. Man, with you on the field, the football team is going
> to be the best it's ever been.

> STEVE
> I can't believe you're saying this.

> CLINT
> It's true.

> STEVE
> But you're captain. And I've never even tried out for anything
> before.

> CLINT
> You're a natural.

> STEVE
> Thanks. Okay there's one more thing I
> want to do before we go home.

> CLINT
> You name it. I'm game.

> STEVE
> Watch this. Now be honest. Tell me what you really think.

> CLINT
> What are you going to do?

Sensational Comedic Scenes: (Two Kids)

                    STEVE
You'll see.

STEVE TAKES A POSE OF A CHEERLEADER.

                    STEVE (cont'd)
(Cheering) "Go team, go. Hit 'em hard. Hit 'em high. We're
going to knock them bye bye bye. Goooooo team."

CLINT IS STUNNED.

                    STEVE (cont'd)
Well, what do you think?

                    CLINT
(Horrified) About what?

                    STEVE
My cheer. I made up a couple more but that's really my best.

                    CLINT
Why are you making up cheers?

                    STEVE
For the tryouts.

                    CLINT
Oh no. Don't tell me.

                    STEVE
What?

                    CLINT
You're not trying out for the football team are you?

                    STEVE
Why would I want to try out for the football team?
All that hitting and smashing into each other.

                    CLINT
YOU WANT TO BE A CHEERLEADER?!!!

                    STEVE
Yeah. Why do you think I asked for your help?

                    CLINT
'Cause I thought you wanted to be on the team.

                    STEVE
(Laughing) No, I just want to cheer for the team.

28   **The Scene Study-guide for Young Actors!**
          Copyright © 2004 by Chambers Stevens

CLINT
But you're so fast. You'd be a great football player.

STEVE
But I really want to be a cheerleader. Now what did you think of my cheer? Am I a natural?

CLINT
You want me to be honest?

STEVE
Yeah.

CLINT
You look like a football player trying to cheer.

STEVE
Really?

CLINT
You're horrible.

STEVE STARTS TO CRY.

CLINT (cont'd)
I'm sorry man, you're just not a good cheerleader.

STEVE
(Crying really hard) But I've been working so hard. I've already made up twenty-five cheers.

CLINT
Okay, okay, stop crying.

STEVE
(A big cry) But I want to cheer.

CLINT
Okay. Just stop crying. I'll help you out.

STEVE
You will?

CLINT
Yeah. I guess. When are the tryouts?

STEVE
Tomorrow.

CLINT
All right. Look, when you do your cheer, you need to be looser. You are way too stiff.

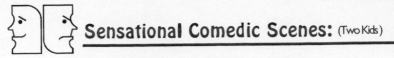
Sensational Comedic Scenes: (Two Kids)

STEVE
What do you mean loose?

CLINT
Like this.

CLINT STANDS AND TAKES A CHEERLEADER POSE.

STEVE
That looks good. But, how do I cheer and be loose at the same time?

CLINT
(Embarrassed) Well, I guess like this. (Clint starts to cheer. He's pretty good) "Go team, go. Hit 'em hard. Hit 'em high. We're going to knock them bye bye bye. Goooooo team."

STEVE
(Stands up and starts clapping) That was great. (Shaking Clint's hand) Well, I've got to go. Thanks for your help.

CLINT
You feel better?

STEVE
Yeah a lot better. I just won twenty-five dollars.

CLINT
What do you mean?

STEVE
(Pointing offstage) See those guys way over there. That's your buddies on the football team. I bet them I could make you do a cheer in the middle of the football field. See you around Clint, ole buddy.

STEVE RUNS OFF.

CLINT
You better run!

CLINT RUNS AFTER HIM.

Get A Job

INT. AVERY'S ROOM

AVERY AND ERIN ARE BROTHER AND SISTER.

           ERIN
No!
           AVERY
Yes!
           ERIN
No!!
           AVERY
Yes!!!
           ERIN
No!!!
           AVERY
Yes!!! Just like that!
           ERIN
Just like that? Mom told you, you have to get a job?
           AVERY
Yes!
           ERIN
No!
           AVERY
Yes!!
           ERIN
Okay, I believe you. But why?
           AVERY
She says I eat too much. She said her and dad can't afford the grocery bill any longer and I have to get a job.
           ERIN
But you're a kid. What can you do to earn money?
           AVERY
Mom called Dr. Sullenger and...
           ERIN
The veterinarian?

Sensational Comedic Scenes: (Two Kids)

                    AVERY
Yes and Dr. Sullenger said I could have a job cleaning...
                    ERIN
Don't tell me!
                    AVERY
...the animal cages!!!
                    ERIN
No!
                    AVERY
Yes!
                    ERIN
That's disgusting!
                    AVERY
Tell me about it. Remember when we brought Butterball there?
That place had tons of cats and dogs. There must be a
thousand cages.
                    ERIN
Well, at least you're going to lose your appetite.

The Scene Study-guide for Young Actors!
Copyright © 2004 by Chambers Stevens

Marry Me

<u>EXT. IN FRONT OF THE SCHOOL</u>

LAUREN IS SITTING ON A SCHOOL BENCH READING HER
HISTORY BOOK. TRAVIS RUNS IN.

>   TRAVIS
> Oh, there you are.

>   LAUREN
> Hey, Travis. You been looking for me?

>   TRAVIS
> Yeah, all day. I've got something really important to ask you.

>   LAUREN
> Okay, what is it?

>   TRAVIS
> (Getting down on one knee) Will you marry me?

>   LAUREN
> (Shocked) What!

>   TRAVIS
> I'm asking you to be my wife.

>   LAUREN
> What are you crazy? Get out of here. We're just kids.
> Kids don't get married.

>   TRAVIS
> Oh, so now you want a divorce? Fine. My lawyer will call
> you in the morning.

TRAVIS STARTS TO LEAVE.

>   LAUREN
> (Grabbing him) Wait! We can't get a divorce 'cause
> we were never married.

>   TRAVIS
> (Turning to Lauren) Exactly. So marry me. And if in a couple of
> months it doesn't work out, then we'll talk about splitting up.

>   LAUREN
> Travis, you're not listening to me. We can't get married...

                    TRAVIS
Moo!

                    LAUREN
What are you doing?

                    TRAVIS
Nothing. You were saying?

                    LAUREN
I was saying we're kids and...

                    TRAVIS
Moo!

                    LAUREN
Why are you doing that?

                    TRAVIS
What?

                    LAUREN
"Mooing." Why are you "mooing"?

                    TRAVIS
(Confused) "Mooing"? You mean like a cow?

                    LAUREN
(Getting upset) Yes, like a cow. Why are you doing that?

                    TRAVIS
Lauren, I think you better sit down. You're hearing things.

                    LAUREN
I'm not hearing things! First, you asked me to marry you and
then you started mooing.

                    TRAVIS
Asked you to marry me? What are you, crazy? I'm a kid.
Kids don't get married.

                    LAUREN
That's what I was trying to tell you.

                    TRAVIS
(Mocking her) "That's what I was trying to tell you."

                    LAUREN
Why are you doing that?

                    TRAVIS
"Why are you doing that?"

LAUREN

Stop it!

TRAVIS

"Stop it!"

LAUREN

Travis!!!!

TRAVIS

Yeah?

LAUREN

Stop it! Stop repeating everything I say.

TRAVIS

I'm not repeating...Lauren, I think you need to sit down.

LAUREN

(Sitting down) Maybe you're right. I don't feel so good.

TRAVIS

You don't look so good. (Jumping back) What is that growing out of your head? Oh no, it's a giant beanstalk. Ah!!!!!!!!!!

LAUREN

(Jumping up and down) Ah!!!!!!!!!!!

TRAVIS

(Trying to calm her down.) Lauren. Lauren. Stop it!

LAUREN

Get it off! Get it off!!!

TRAVIS

LAUREN!!! Why are you screaming?

LAUREN

The beanstalk! Get it off!

TRAVIS

Lauren what are you talking about? I don't see any beanstalk.

LAUREN

(Still upset) You just said it was growing out of my head.

TRAVIS

I said what? I think you need to lie down.

LAUREN

(Lying down) Okay, I have a headache.

TRAVIS

Maybe you should call your mother and tell her to come get you.

LAUREN
Yeah. You're right. But I have to turn in my history homework.

TRAVIS
Oh, I'll turn it in for you.

LAUREN
(Starting to exit) Thanks. I'm going to the office to call my mom. Please don't forget to turn it in.

LAUREN EXITS.

TRAVIS
I won't. But first I have to copy all of your answers.
(He laughs a big, wicked laugh) She is such a sucker.

Missing

EXT. A DESERT ISLAND

HALLIE AND IVY ARE SITTING ON THE SAND.

> HALLIE
> Of all the stupid ideas.

> IVY
> How was I to know the boat was going to sink?

> HALLIE
> For one thing, you could have checked to see if we had enough gas.

> IVY
> Look, we're going to be rescued soon so let's just make the best of it.

> HALLIE
> Rescued? How do you know?

> IVY
> Because our parents will realize we're missing, and they'll send the Coast Guard out to look for us.

> HALLIE
> That's what everyone on Gilligan's Island thought, too.

> IVY
> Don't say that.

> HALLIE
> It's true. Face facts. We're in big trouble.

> IVY
> No, we're not. We'll just make an SOS sign, and when a plane flies over they'll see us.

> HALLIE
> Okay. You get some rocks and I'll make the sign.

> IVY
> (Looking around) There's no rocks. We're on a beach.

> HALLIE
> Shoot. Hey, how about if we spell it in the sand?

> IVY
> Good idea. (Starts writing in the sand) "Dear Plane, My name is Ivy and my friend's name is..."

Copyright © 2004 by Chambers Stevens

> HALLIE
(Stomping on her writing) You don't need to write a whole letter.
Just write "Help!"

IVY WRITES "HELP" IN THE SAND.

> IVY
I'm hungry.

> HALLIE
Me, too.

> IVY
I bet our parents are just sitting down to breakfast.

> HALLIE
Yeah.

> IVY
They're probably eating eggs and bacon and toast and pancakes.

> HALLIE
Stop it! You're going to make me crazy.

> IVY
I'm hungry.

> HALLIE
Maybe we should look around for some food.

> IVY
Like what?

> HALLIE
I don't know. On Gilligan's Island they were always
eating coconuts.

> IVY
There's some trees over there. I'll go look.

> HALLIE
Okay. I'll stay on the lookout for planes.

IVY EXITS. HALLIE CONTINUES WRITING "HELP" IN THE SAND.
AFTER A BEAT IVY ENTERS EATING A POPSICLE.

> IVY
I couldn't find any coconuts.

The Scene Study-guide for Young Actors!

HALLIE

Where did you get that popsicle?

IVY

There's a restaurant behind those trees. This nice man just gave it to me. He said there's a big hotel up the hill. Maybe we can go there if we get tired. (She sits down) I hope we get rescued soon. Have you seen any planes?

HALLIE

(Grabbing the popsicle) Oh, brother.

Not My Fault

<u>INT. THE HALL OUTSIDE THE PRINCIPAL'S OFFICE</u>

SYBIL IS WAITING WHEN MICHELLE WALKS UP.

> SYBIL
> I didn't tell.

> MICHELLE
> Oh, please!

> SYBIL
> Michelle, I didn't, I swear.

> MICHELLE
> Then why does Principal Cathcart want to see us?

> SYBIL
> I didn't tell!

> MICHELLE
> Sybil, you have the biggest mouth in school. Everybody knows it. You had to have told someone.

> SYBIL
> I didn't.

> MICHELLE
> Not anyone?

> SYBIL
> Well, I told Margaret, but she wouldn't have told anyone.

> MICHELLE
> MARGARET JOHNSON?!!! Are you crazy?
> Remember last year when I told her about Bobby liking me and she told the whole school?

> SYBIL
> Whoops, I forgot about that.

> MICHELLE
> We're in big trouble.

> SYBIL
> No, we're not. I'll go right in there and tell Principal Cathcart it was all my fault.

> MICHELLE
> Like he would believe you. He knows how smart I am. He'll know it was my idea.

                    SYBIL
Well, it was your idea.

                    MICHELLE
AND NO ONE WOULD HAVE KNOWN ABOUT IT
IF YOU WOULD HAVE KEPT YOUR BIG MOUTH SHUT!!

                    SYBIL
Sometimes you can be mean.

                    MICHELLE
Look, we have to come up with a plan.
Otherwise we're in big trouble.

A BEAT.

                    SYBIL
I've got it. Let's tell the truth.

                    MICHELLE
Are you nuts?

                    SYBIL
It just might work. Think about it. We walk in there and say,
"Okay, you caught us. We admit it. We did it."

                    MICHELLE
He'd be shocked.

                    SYBIL
Right. Then before he has time to recover we say, "Michelle and I
were just sitting around one day talking about how much we like
you. We were talking about how funny you are. And what a great
sense of humor you have. And then Michelle said, 'Let's play a
practical joke on Principal Cathcart to show him how much we
like him,' and I thought that was a great idea. Because, look at
your office. You've won all kinds of awards for being a great
principal. But I bet no one's given you a practical joke for doing a
good job."

                    MICHELLE
Yeah, and then I'll say, "So then we got some poster board and
we made tons of signs that read, PRINCIPAL CATHCART
WEARS A TOUPEE. And PRINCIPAL CATHCART
HAS BAD BREATH. And then we got to school one morning
really early."

SYBIL
"It was dark outside."

                    MICHELLE
"Yeah, and we put them up all over the school. So we hope you
appreciate all the time and effort we put into your
joke. It was a lot of hard work."

                    SYBIL
"But it was our pleasure because we like you?"

                    MICHELLE
Don't say like. Say respect you.

                    SYBIL
Good idea. "..but it was our pleasure because we respect you.
And by the way your new toupee really hides your bald spot."
That's it! Think it will work?

A BEAT. THEY LOOK AT EACH OTHER.

                    MICHELLE
He's gonna kill us.

                    SYBIL
Pretty much.

Off With Her Head

INT. PRINCESS BETSY'S ROOM IN THE CASTLE

PRINCESS BETSY IS READING WHEN HER SERVANT MEESA ENTERS.

> MEESA
> Your Majesty?

> PRINCESS BETSY
> Yes?

> MEESA
> The Queen wants me to remind you that the Prince of Za is coming to dinner tonight.

> PRINCESS BETSY
> Oh, not that bore!

> MEESA
> Should I tell the Queen that you won't be coming?

> PRINCESS BETSY
> No. She'll just send the guards up here to drag me to dinner. I can't stand the Prince of Za. He is soooooooo boring!

> MEESA
> His servants are soooooooooooo boring, too.

> PRINCESS BETSY
> Really?

> MEESA
> Yes, your Majesty. They go on and on about how great the Prince of Za is.

> PRINCESS BETSY
> They're wrong. Meesa, what am I to do?

> MEESA
> You could sneak out of the castle.

> PRINCESS BETSY
> No. Last time I did that Father sent the dragon after me.

> MEESA
> You could pretend you're sick.

> PRINCESS BETSY
> Then Mother would just send the wizard up here to make me better.

Copyright © 2004 by Chambers Stevens

MEESA
Then I don't know. Maybe you'll just
have to have dinner with the Prince of Za.

PRINCESS BETSY
I can't do that! He's in love with me. If I keep having dinner
with him, the Queen will force me to marry him.

MEESA
What you need is a double.

PRINCESS BETSY
A what?

MEESA
A double, your Majesty. Someone to pretend to be you.

PRINCESS BETSY
That would never work. Where would I ever find someone to
pretend to...wait I've got it. (Hugging Meesa) You're a genius.

MEESA
What did I do?

PRINCESS BETSY
You'll be my double!

MEESA
I can't do that!

PRINCESS BETSY
You'll do it or I'll chop off your head.

MEESA
Well, since you put it that way...

PRINCESS BETSY
That's my girl. Put on one of my dresses. Get a veil to cover your
face. Then when it's time for dinner you'll go as me.

MEESA
Do you really think this will work?

PRINCESS BETSY
It better work or I'll cut off your legs.

MEESA
It'll work!

PRINCESS BETSY
That's my girl. Now get dressed.

Pirates

EXT. THE DECK OF A PIRATE SHIP

CAPTAIN BOY IS TIED TO THE MAST OF THE SHIP. SWEENY IS
STANDING GUARD.

> CAPTAIN BOY
> (Very angry) Shoot. Shoot. Shoot.

> SWEENY
> Excuse me, did you say something?

> CAPTAIN BOY
> Yes, matey. I said, "Shoot. Shoot. Shoot."

> SWEENY
> That's what I thought you said.

> CAPTAIN BOY
> I can't believe it. Me, Captain Boy, the youngest, bravest
> pirate to ever sail the seven seas has been captured by you.
> What's your name?

> SWEENY
> Sweeny, sir.

> CAPTAIN BOY
> By Sweeny, the dumbest pirate to ever sail the seven seas.

> SWEENY
> I can't believe I captured you either. But hey, all I had to do was
> sneak up behind you, and bam, you were caught.

> CAPTAIN BOY
> Don't remind me. When does the rest of your ship return?

> SWEENY
> They went to the island to pick up supplies. Boy, when they get
> back and see what I've done, I bet they'll make me first mate.

> CAPTAIN BOY
> First mate? Sweeny, I am the greatest pirate who has ever lived.
> They'll make you captain for sure.

> SWEENY
> But we've already got a captain.

> CAPTAIN BOY
> Oh, they'll probably kill him, and you'll take his place.

SWEENY
They'll kill Captain Frank? But he's such a nice guy.

CAPTAIN BOY
Nice? Captains aren't supposed to be nice.

SWEENY
Well, Captain Frank is. He always gives me candy.
And once, when I got seasick, he let me have some medicine to
keep me from barfing all over the deck.

CAPTAIN BOY
On my ships, if a guy gets seasick, we just toss him over the side.

SWEENY
But Captain Frank's different. He's a real sweetie.

CAPTAIN BOY
Well, a sweetie or not, they'll kill him and put you in charge.

SWEENY STARTS TO UNTIE CAPTAIN BOY.

CAPTAIN BOY (cont'd)
What are you doing?

SWEENY
(Finishing untying him) Go on, get out of here.

CAPTAIN BOY
You're just letting me go?

SWEENY
Go on, scoot. I like Captain Frank. I don't want him to die.

CAPTAIN BOY
Sweeny, you are truly the dumbest man on the sea. Now,
if you'll just give me back my sword I'll be on my way.

SWEENY BENDS DOWN TO PICK UP THE CAPTAIN'S SWORD. AT
THE SAME TIME, THE CAPTAIN BENDS DOWN TO STRAIGHTEN HIS
BOOT. SWEENY TURNS AROUND AND ACCIDENTALLY RUNS THE
SWORD THROUGH THE CAPTAIN.

CAPTAIN BOY (cont'd)
Ooooooooooo. No. You've got me.

THE CAPTAIN DOES A BIG DEATH SCENE AND THEN
DIES ON THE DECK.

SWEENY
Oh, no. Looks like I'm going to be captain.

The Salesman

INT. THE SCHOOL HALLWAY

MIKIE IS PUTTING HIS BOOKS IN HIS LOCKER WHEN
BRET WALKS UP.

                    BRET
        Hey, partner! How are you doing?

                    MIKIE
        Do I know you?

                    BRET
        Not yet, but I can tell that soon we are going to be
        the best of friends.

                    MIKIE
        Look, I'm late for class and—

                    BRET
        (Grabbing Mikie's arm) What class do you have?

                    MIKIE
        Math. Mrs. Piedmont.

                    BRET
        Oh, she's really tough!

                    MIKIE
        Right, and I can't be late cause I'm not doing too good and...

                    BRET
        That, friend, is why you need me. So what kind of grades
        are you making, B's, C's?

                    MIKIE
        Worse. Now look I have to get to...

                    BRET
        D's? Man, that's terrible. Buddy, you are dumber than
        you look. But no need to worry, I can help you out.
        First, do you have any money?

                    MIKIE
        A couple of dollars for lunch.

                    BRET
        Let me see it.

MIKIE
(Taking out his money) It's my lunch money.

BRET
(Grabbing the money) Okay, it's not much but it will get you started. Now close your eyes and repeat after me...

MIKIE
What, are you some kind of nut? Give me back my money.

BRET
Do you want to keep getting D's in math?

MIKIE
No.

BRET
Then close your eyes.

MIKIE
(He does) This is so stupid. I'm going to be late.

BRET
Yeah, yeah, yeah. Now repeat after me. "Igapod. Beanbag. Ram rod."

MIKIE
Igapod. Beanbag. Ram rod.

BRET
"Pizza, bananas, and cheese."

MIKIE
Pizza, bananas, and Cheese."

BRET
Okay, you can open your eyes now.

MIKIE
(Opening his eyes) That's it? What was that, some kind of spell?

BRET
That's right, you are now a math genius! Congratulations. Now I have to get going. I have a big test in history.

MIKIE
(Grabbing Bret) Look buddy, give me back my money or I'm going to make you wish...

BRET
Oh, you think now that you're a genius, you can push us little guys around?

MIKIE
I'm not a genius.

BRET
Really? What's seventy-five times nine hundred and seventy-seven?

MIKIE
Seventy-three thousand, two hundred and
seventy-five! How did I know that?

BRET
I told you, you're a genius. What's seven million times four
hundred and thirty-six.

MIKIE
Three billion and fifty-two million.

BRET
Right!

MIKIE
I am a genius!

BRET
Now, run to class, this spell only works for twenty-five minutes.
And you've only got twenty-four more to go.

MIKIE
(Giving him a big hug) Thanks a ton. How can I ever thank you?

BRET
Easy. Bring more money tomorrow. See you, pal.
Good luck in class.

MIKIE
I don't need luck. I'm a genius!

MIKIE RUNS OFF.

BRET
I forgot to tell him that the spell turns him into a monkey at
midnight. Oh, well, he'll find out soon enough.
(Seeing another kid by his locker) Hey, partner.
How are you doing?

The Secret

INT. LISA'S ROOM

LISA IS SITTING ON THE FLOOR DOING HER HOMEWORK WHEN SEAN RUNS IN.

> **SEAN**
> (Teasing her) Ha, ha, ha, ha, ha. I know a secret, and you don't know it.

> **LISA**
> Well, I don't care.

> **SEAN**
> Oh, if you knew it, you would.

> **LISA**
> I don't care.

> **SEAN**
> Yes, you do!

> **LISA**
> No, I don't.

> **SEAN**
> Okay. Then I'm leaving.

> **LISA**
> Go!

> **SEAN**
> But if I walk out of this room, I am never ever ever telling you the secret.

> **LISA**
> For the millionth time, I don't care.

> **SEAN**
> (Starting to walk out) I'm leaving.

> **LISA**
> I'm glad.

> **SEAN**
> I'm glad you're glad.

SEAN LEAVES. A BEAT. SEAN REENTERS.

SEAN (cont'd)
(Begging) Come on, don't you want to know?

                    LISA
No! No! No! Can't you see I'm doing my
homework? I don't have time for your stupid games.

                    SEAN
It's a good secret.

                    LISA
Look, will you leave if I let you tell me your stupid secret?

                    SEAN
Yes.

                    LISA
You promise?

                    SEAN
Promise.

                    LISA
Okay, what is it?

A BEAT.

                    SEAN
I forgot.

LISA STANDS UP AND PUSHES SEAN OUT OF THE ROOM.

Space Race

<u>EXT. A RACE TRACK</u>

THE 23RD CENTURY. ERATO IS IN HIS SPACESHIP WHEN IBOD
PULLS UP IN HIS NEW AR93.

> IBOD
> Hey, sucker. Are you ready to lose today?

> ERATO
> Oh, no! Don't tell me you're in this race, too.

> IBOD
> Erato, you don't stand a chance. Last week I got a new
> hyper-drive on this baby. She can go from zero to one
> million in three seconds.

> ERATO
> Sounds like you got a hyper-drive for your mouth, too.

> IBOD
> Yeah, we'll see who's so smart when I win this race and become
> the pod champion of the galaxy.

> ERATO
> Yeah, right. That will never happen.

> IBOD
> Look, here comes the guy with the starting pistol.
> See you at the finish line, sucker.

> BOTH
> Three! Two. One. Blast off!

BOTH SPACESHIPS DON'T MOVE.

> ERATO
> What happened?

> IBOD
> Come on you piece of junk. Go!!!!

> ERATO
> (Looking at his gauge) Out of fuel?
> How can I be out of fuel?

> IBOD
> Maybe somebody emptied your uranium tank.

ERATO
What!? You're a scum!

IBOD
(Looking at his dashboard) How come my hyper-drive isn't working?

ERATO
(Holding up a wire) Maybe somebody stole your plutonium cable!

IBOD
(Jumping out of his ship) Give it to me.

ERATO
Not till you give me back my uranium.

IBOD
I can't. I put it in my tank.

ERATO
Then no plutonium cable.

IBOD
Okay. Okay. Look, how about if we team up.

ERATO
With you? Never!

IBOD
Then you're going to lose. We both can ride in my ship since it's already full of fuel.

ERATO
Which you stole.

IBOD
Come on, let's team up?

ERATO
But who gets to fly?

IBOD
Me. It's my ship.

ERATO
Then forget it.

IBOD
Okay. We'll both fly.

ERATO
(Handing him the cable as he gets in the cockpit) I've always wanted to fly one of these babies.

Sensational Comedic Scenes: (Two Kids)

IBOD
(Smelling Erato) Man, did you take a shower today?

ERATO
On my planet, we don't believe in showers.

IBOD
(Holding his nose) I can tell. Let's go.

ERATO AND IBOD TAKE OFF TO WIN THE RACE.

Space School

INT. INSIDE A SPACESHIP

WIGET, A ROBOT, IS AT THE STEERING CONSOLE WHEN KATIE
ENTERS.

>   KATIE
> Excuse me, is this spaceship number seven thousand five
> hundred and eleven?

>   WIGET
> (In her best robot voice) Affirmative.

>   KATIE
> Great! I've been up and down the loading dock looking
> for this ship. Oh, excuse me, I'm so rude. My name is Katie.

>   WIGET
> This fact is already knowledge to me.

>   KATIE
> You know you talk kind of funny. What are you,
> some kind of robot?

>   WIGET
> Affirmative. I am a model XL-6400.

>   KATIE
> Cool. I've never met a robot before.

>   WIGET
> (Getting excited) Ooo, my sensors tell me it is now
> eleven o'clock. Your first flying lesson will now begin.

>   KATIE
> Out of sight. Where do I sit?

>   WIGET
> This is the steering console. Please place yourself behind it.

>   KATIE
> (Sitting) Wow, look at all these buttons. There must be almost a
> thousand of them.

>   WIGET
> Eleven hundred and eighty. But don't worry, you don't have to
> memorize them all on your first day. Now before we
> start do you have any questions?

Sensational Comedic Scenes: (Two Kids)

KATIE
Yeah. What is this big red button here?

KATIE PUSHES THE BUTTON. THE SPACESHIP TAKES OFF AT THE SPEED OF LIGHT.

WIGET
Ahhhhhh!!! Help we are going to die!!!!

KATIE
(Trying to steer the ship) Oh no!!! Help!!!!!

WIGET REACHES OVER AND PUSHES THE BUTTON. THE SHIP STOPS.

KATIE (cont'd)
(Hugging Wiget) Thank you, thank you, you've saved my life.

WIGET
Actually, I was playing a joke on you. The best thing about the XL-6400's is we have a sense of humor.

KATIE
It wasn't all that funny.

WIGET
(Laughing) You should have seen your face.

KATIE
Whatever. Can we start my lesson now?

WIGET
Affirmative. Okay, the first thing you need to remember is never, ever, ever push this blue button.

WIGET POINTS TO THE BLUE BUTTON.

KATIE
You're just saying that because you want me to push it.

WIGET
Actually, the chances of you pushing it are seven thousand and forty-three to one. Which means that you have learned your lesson. And you will never disobey me ever again.

KATIE
Oh, yeah? So you think you know everything?

WIGET
I am an XL-6400.

Sensational Comedic Scenes: (Two Kids)

KATIE
(Pushing the button) Then did you know I was going to do this?

THE SHIP STARTS TO SHAKE.

WIGET
You shouldn't have done that.

KATIE
Why?

WIGET
Because in ten seconds, you are going
to be ejected from your seat.

KATIE
Sure I am. I'm not falling for that again.

KATIE IS EJECTED FROM HER SEAT!

WIGET
How come humans never listen?

Yearbook

INT. THE LUNCH ROOM

TOM IS EATING WHEN JULIANNE WALKS UP.

>   JULIANNE
> Excuse me.

>   TOM
> Yeah?

>   JULIANNE
> Will you sign my yearbook?

>   TOM
> (Looking around) Are you talking to me?

>   JULIANNE
> Yeah. Tom, right?

>   TOM
> Yeah. Have we met?

>   JULIANNE
> No. Well, not officially. But once in seventh grade, you bumped
> into me and said, "Excuse me."

>   TOM
> Oh.

>   JULIANNE
> I remembered that because not many guys around here are polite.

>   TOM
> I've noticed that, too.

>   JULIANNE
> So, will you sign it?

>   TOM
> Yeah, I guess.

JULIANNE HANDS TOM HER YEARBOOK.

>   TOM (cont'd)
> What's your name?

>   JULIANNE
> Julianne.

TOM
Pretty name.

JULIANNE
I knew you would say that.

TOM
You did?

JULIANNE
Yeah. 'Cause you're polite.

TOM
Right. (Opening the yearbook) Where do
you want me to sign it?

JULIANNE
(Grabbing the yearbook) Page fifty-four. That's your Math Club
picture. (Changing her mind) No, no, on page sixty-three, your
Science club photo is much better. No wait, better sign on page
ninety-seven.

TOM
What am I doing on page ninety-seven?

JULIANNE
It's the picture of you winning the chess tournament.

TOM
That was a great match.

JULIANNE
Yeah. When you sacrificed your knight everyone was surprised.

TOM
(Laughing) Yeah, Tommy Bagwell never even saw it coming.

JULIANNE
(Laughing) He thought he was so smart
with his little pawn decoy move.

TOM
(Laughing) Please, like I didn't see that coming.

JULIANNE
Yeah. Even I saw that.

THEY LAUGH HYSTERICALLY. TOM THEN STOPS AND STARES
STRAIGHT INTO JULIANNE'S EYES. THERE IS A MOMENT OF LOVE
BETWEEN THEM.

> TOM
> You sure know a lot about chess.

> JULIANNE
> Well, I've watched all your tournaments. You're a great teacher.

> TOM
> How come you didn't introduce yourself to me before today?

> JULIANNE
> I didn't want you to think I was stupid.

> TOM
> How could anybody think you're stupid?

> JULIANNE
> You'd be surprised.

THEY STARE INTO EACH OTHER'S EYES FOR A BEAT LONGER.
THEN, JULIANNE EMBARRASSED, TURNS AWAY.

> JULIANNE (cont'd)
> (Handing him the yearbook) Oh, here.

> TOM
> Oh, right.

TOM SIGNS IT. THEN HANDS IT BACK.

> TOM (cont'd)
> I didn't bring my yearbook to school
> today. You could have signed mine.

> JULIANNE
> No!

> TOM
> Sure, why not?

> JULIANNE
> Gosh. (Getting nervous) Okay. Well, thanks. I better go.

> TOM
> (Stopping her) Wait.

> JULIANNE
> Yeah?

> TOM
> Nice meeting you.

> JULIANNE
> Me, too.

JULIANNE TURNS TO LEAVE.

> TOM
> Wait.

> JULIANNE
> (Turning around) Yeah?

> TOM
> What's your last name?

> JULIANNE
> Lane. Like a street. But smaller.

> TOM
> Julianne Lane. Pretty name.

> JULIANNE
> Thank you. You're so polite.

JULIANNE TURNS TO LEAVE AGAIN.

> TOM
> Julianne?

> JULIANNE
> Yeah?

> TOM
> Maybe I could bring my yearbook over to your house
> so you could sign it?

> JULIANNE
> Really?

> TOM
> Sure. Then maybe we could go to a movie or something.

> JULIANNE
> A new Star Trek opens tomorrow.

> TOM
> (Excited) You like Star Trek?

> JULIANNE
> Love it. Almost as much as Star Wars.

> TOM
> You like Star Wars, too?

> JULIANNE
> I have pictures of Chewbacca all over my wall.

TOM
Me, too.

JULIANNE
No!

TOM
Yes. That and Princess Leia.

JULIANNE
She's very pretty.

TOM
Not as pretty as you.

THEY STARE AT EACH OTHER FOR ANOTHER BEAT. THEY ARE OBVIOUSLY IN LOVE.

JULIANNE
(Not moving) Well, I better go.

TOM
(Not moving) Yeah me, too.

JULIANNE
I can't move.

TOM
Me either. It feels like I'm in a Vulcan death grip.

JULIANNE
You think this is what love feels like?

TOM
Must be.

JULIANNE
Feels pretty good.

TOM
Yeah. It's even better than chess.

Sensational Comedic Scenes: (Three Kids)

Bullies

EXT. THE PARK

LEN IS SITTING ON A PARK BENCH READING WHEN BUD AND
SPIKE ENTER.

             SPIKE
Hey kid, what are you reading?

             LEN
It's a history book for class.

             BUD
(Grabbing and reading the book) "George Washington?"
What a doofus. Hey, Spike! Look how ole George is wearing a wig.

             SPIKE
George must be a girl. 'Cause only girls wear wigs.

             LEN
Can I have my book back now?

             SPIKE
I don't know. What do you think Bud?
Should we give him back his girl book?

             BUD
I say...no!

             LEN
Come on.

             BUD
No! Unless, the little dweeb gets on his knees and begs.

             SPIKE
Yeah. If you want your book back you have to either get on your
knees and beg or...give us a million dollars!

             BUD
Yeah, a million dollars!

             LEN
Look guys, just give me back my book and there won't be trouble.

             SPIKE
Listen to this squirt. Are you threatening us?

             BUD
'Cause if you are, we're going to smash your face.

Sensational Scenes for Kids **63**

LEN
No. I'm not threatening you. I just want my book back.

SPIKE
Are you going to beg?

LEN
No.

BUD
Then you owe us a million dollars.

SPIKE
Yeah, a million dollars!

LEN
(Taking off his coat) I didn't want to have to do this but...

SPIKE
What are you doing?

LEN
I'm going to get my book back.

BUD
Listen to this kid. He thinks he's bad.

LEN
I'm not bad. But I am a black belt in karate. I was taught never to hurt anyone.

LEN GETS IN A KARATE POSE.

LEN (cont'd)
But you've left me no choice.

SPIKE
(Laughing) Oooooo scary.

BUD AND SPIKE TAKE FIGHTING STANCES.

BUD
Yeah little guy, let us know when you're ready to fight.

SPIKE
Yeah. Let us know.

LEN GOES CRAZY WITH HIS KARATE MOVES.

LEN
(Making wild noises) Ah. Yah. Eee yah.

SPIKE
(Scared) Let's get out of here before he kills us.

BUD
Run.

SPIKE AND BUD RUN. THEY ALSO DROP THE BOOK.

LEN
(Picking up the book) Sorry George. I know you never told a lie. But I had to lie about the karate or I would have never gotten you back.

LEN SITS DOWN AND READS.

Drums

<u>INT. INSIDE TOMMY'S GARAGE</u>

TOMMY, JAMIE, AND BRET ARE ALL PLAYING DRUMS IN A BAND.

> TOMMY
> One, two, three, four.

JAMIE, BRET, AND TOMMY START PLAYING THEIR DRUMS AT THE SAME TIME. IT SOUNDS REALLY BAD.

> TOMMY (cont'd)
> Stop! Stop! That sounds horrible.

> JAMIE
> We need a guitar player.

> BRET
> And a singer.

> TOMMY
> No, we don't! Every rock band has a guitar player and a singer.

> JAMIE
> That's why we need them, too.

> TOMMY
> We should be different. We'll be the first band in the world to just have drums.

> BRET
> But it sounds horrible.

> TOMMY
> We just need to practice some more.
> Okay here goes. One, two, three, four.

AGAIN THEY PLAY AND AGAIN IT SOUNDS HORRIBLE.

> TOMMY (cont'd)
> Stop! Stop! Jamie, you and Bret are playing off beat.

> JAMIE
> We're playing together. I think you're the one off beat.

> TOMMY
> How can I be off beat, if I'm the one doing the counting?

> BRET
> Don't ask us but you're the one off beat.

The Scene Study-guide for Young Actors!
Copyright © 2004 by Chambers Stevens

Sensational Comedic Scenes: (Three Kids)

TOMMY
Okay, let's try it again. One, two, three, four.

IT SOUNDS WORSE THIS TIME.

TOMMY (cont'd)
Stop! Stop! Something's wrong. It sounds worse than ever.

BRET
We need a guitar player.

JAMIE
And a singer.

TOMMY
Look guys, we are not putting guitars or singers in this band.

JAMIE
How come you never listen to our ideas?

TOMMY
Because I'm the leader of the band, that's why. Wait, I've got an idea. (He puts his drum down and walks over to a box on the floor) This is perfect. (Pulling them out of the box) Blindfolds.

BRET
Blindfolds?

TOMMY
Yeah, our problem is we're watching instead of listening to each other. (Handing out the blindfolds) Now here put these on.

TOMMY PUTS HIS ON BUT JAMIE AND BRET DON'T.

TOMMY (cont'd)
Have you got them on?

BRET
(Lying) Yeah.

JAMIE
(Trying not to laugh) Yep.

TOMMY
Good, now let's starts. One, two, three, four.

TOMMY STARTS TO PLAY DRUMS. THE OTHER TWO GUYS LOOK AT EACH OTHER AND THEN EXIT.

TOMMY (cont'd)
Now that sounds much better. I told you we don't need anything but drums.

Dumped

INT. INSIDE DIANE'S HOUSE

DIANE, JOANIE, AND ASHLEY ARE JUST SITTING, STARING AT THE WALL.

>   DIANE
> I am soooooo bored.

>   JOANIE
> Yep.

>   ASHLEY
> What can we do?

>   JOANIE
> We could watch TV.

>   ASHLEY
> Nah. There's nothing good on Monday nights.

>   DIANE
> We could bake some cookies.

>   JOANIE
> Nah. Last time we did that we burned them and
> your mom made us scrub the baking pans.

>   DIANE
> That was a bummer.

>   ASHLEY
> Yeah.

>   JOANIE
> Hey, how about we make some prank calls!

>   DIANE
> No. Everybody we know has caller ID.

>   ASHLEY
> Yeah, what is the point of making prank calls if the people
> you're calling already know who you are?

>   JOANIE
> I guess you're right.

>   DIANE
> I am sooo bored.

>   JOANIE
> You've already said that.

DIANE
Well, I'll say it again.

ASHLEY
Hey, we could go to Joanie's house and pick on her big brother.

JOANIE
He's not at home. He's on a date.

ASHLEY
With who?

JOANIE
Ruth Schmitz.

ASHLEY
You're kidding.

DIANE
Ruth is like the most popular girl in the school.
Why did she want to go out with your brother?

JOANIE
My brother is a good guy.

DIANE
He is not!

ASHLEY
He's always picking on you.

JOANIE
Yeah, but I deserve it. Because I always pick on him first.

DIANE
I still can't believe Ruth is going out with your brother.

JOANIE
She's cool. She was over at the house yesterday and she said
she wants to introduce me to some cool people at school.

ASHLEY AND DIANE LOOK AT ONE ANOTHER.

ASHLEY AND DIANE
Oh, no.

JOANIE
What?

ASHLEY
Now you're going to be popular.

DIANE
Yeah. And you're going to have a whole new group of friends
and never talk to us again.

JOANIE
What are you talking about?

DIANE
Ruth is going to introduce you to all the cool people.
And they're going to like you. And then you'll hang out
with them and...

ASHLEY
...then you'll dump us.

JOANIE
I wouldn't do that. Look how much fun we have together.
Why would I want to dump you guys?

ASHLEY
She's going to dump us.

DIANE
Yep. You're going to dump us.

Haunted House

<u>INT. AN OLD DESERTED HOUSE</u>

SAM, LANE, AND MARTIN ENTER WITH A MOVIE CAMERA.

> SAM
>
> This is freaky.

> LANE
>
> You're telling me.

> MARTIN
>
> Guys, maybe we shouldn't be in here.

> LANE
>
> Why? Are you chicken?

> MARTIN
>
> No. It's just...

> SAM
>
> You're scared.

> MARTIN
>
> Aren't you?

> SAM
>
> No. Now let's get to work. Put the camera over there.

MARTIN SETS UP THE CAMERA.

> LANE
>
> This is a great house for the final scene of our movie.

> SAM
>
> It's perfect. It's going to give our film that extra touch.
> Now lets go over the scene.

> MARTIN
>
> I really don't think we should be in here.

> LANE
>
> Don't start that again.

> MARTIN
>
> What happens if this place is haunted or something?

> LANE
>
> (Laughing) You are such a baby.

> SAM
>
> Martin. it's not haunted! It's just a run-down old house.
> Now lets get to work. Okay, Lane, put on your mask.

LANE PUTS ON A SCARY MASK.

> SAM (cont'd)
>
> Okay, now Martin you come down the stairs and..

JUST THEN A LOUD NOISE IS HEARD FROM OFFSTAGE TOWARDS
THE STAIRS.

> MARTIN
>
> What was that?

> LANE
>
> I didn't hear anything.

> MARTIN
>
> It was loud. (To Sam) Did you hear it?

> LANE
>
> Come on, you guys, it's hot in this mask.

> SAM
>
> It's probably just a mouse or something.

> MARTIN
>
> That didn't sound like a mouse. It sounded more like a giant bear.

> SAM
>
> Look, the sooner we shoot the scene the sooner we can
> get out of here. Now Martin, you come down the stairs.
> Go on get in place.

MARTIN SLOWLY MOVES TOWARD THE STAIRS.

> SAM (cont'd)
>
> And Lane you hide behind the...

AGAIN, THERE IS A LOUD NOISE OFFSTAGE. MARTIN RUNS BACK
TO SAM.

> MARTIN
>
> Now, don't tell me you didn't hear that.

> LANE
>
> I can't hear nothing in this mask.

> **SAM**
> Martin, it's okay. I'm sure it's nothing.

> **MARTIN**
> You mean nothing like a monster? Or do you mean nothing like a murderer?

> **SAM**
> I mean nothing like nothing. Now get by the stairs.

MARTIN GOES BACK TO THE STAIRS.

> **SAM (cont'd)**
> Now Lane, when Martin comes down the stairs you jump out and...

JUST THEN THE NOISE IS HEARD AGAIN.

> **MARTIN**
> (Running off) Sorry, guys, I've got to go. I don't feel like getting killed today.

> **SAM**
> (Grabbing him) Martin! Look it's just a noise. (Dragging him offstage in the direction of the noise) I'll prove to you. Nothing is wrong.

THEY EXIT. A BEAT. THEN THEY RUN BACK IN.

> **MARTIN**
> Run! Lane! Run!

> **SAM**
> (Grabbing the camera) Let's get out of here!!!

SAM AND MARTIN EXIT. LANE IS JUST STANDING THERE IN THE MASK.

> **LANE**
> Are you guys talking to me? It's really hard to hear in here.

THE LOUD NOISE IS AGAIN, BUT THIS TIME IT SAYS, "LOSER!!!"

The Meow

<u>EXT. SHERYL'S FRONT PORCH</u>

SHERYL IS SITTING ON HER FRONT PORCH WHEN GERTIE, THE CAT, WALKS UP.

> GERTIE
>
> Meow.

> SHERYL
>
> Hey, look at you, little kitty. (Petting Gertie) Where did you come from?

> GERTIE
>
> Meow.

> SHERYL
>
> I wonder if you're lost.

> GERTIE
>
> Meow.

> SHERYL
>
> Maybe I should call the pound and see if anyone has lost a kitten.

> GERTIE
>
> You do that and I'll scratch your eyes out.

> SHERYL
>
> What did you say?

> GERTIE
>
> Meow.

> SHERYL
>
> Did you just say something? I must be hearing things.

> GERTIE
>
> Meow.

> SHERYL
>
> I better call the pound before they close.

> GERTIE
>
> You do that and your eyes will be gone for good.

> SHERYL
>
> You're talking!

GERTIE

Meow.

SHERYL

No. I'm sure I heard it this time. Talk again! Come on talk!

GERTIE

Meow.

SHERYL

Not cat language! Speak in human language!!

GERTIE

Meow.

SHERYL

Come on, speak!!!

GERTIE

Meow.

PATTY ENTERS.

PATTY

Sheryl why are you yelling at that cat?

SHERYL

It was talking to me.

PATTY

Talking?

SHERYL

Yeah, it said if I call the pound, it's
going to scratch my eyes out.

PATTY

Sheryl, I think you need to lie down.

SHERYL

I'm serious. Watch this. (To Gertie)
Come on kitty, speak for me.

GERTIE

Meow.

SHERYL

In English.

GERTIE

Meow. Meow. Meow.

PATTY
Sheryl. I think you should go inside and lie down.

SHERYL
Maybe you're right. Will you take care of the cat for me?

PATTY
Whose is it?

SHERYL
I don't know. I think it's a stray.

PATTY
Okay, I'll take care of her. Just go inside and lie down.

SHERYL
Thanks.

SHERYL EXITS.

PATTY
Okay, little kitty, lets go to the
pound and see if anyone has lost you.

GERTIE
Kid, you touch me and I'll rip your hair out.

PATTY
(Exiting) Sheryl, wait up! I need to lie down, too.

PATTY EXITS. GERTIE SITS ON THE FRONT PORCH.

GERTIE
Meow.

Sensational Dramatic Scenes for Kids!

Sensational Dramatic Scenes: (Two Kids)

Divorce

INT. NORA JANE'S BEDROOM

Nora Jane is lying on the bed crying when Suzanne enters.

> SUZANNE
>
> Nora Jane?

Nora Jane looks up and runs to Suzanne who holds her.

> SUZANNE (cont'd)
> (Trying to comfort her) It's okay. It's okay.

> NORA JANE
> My parents are getting a divorce.

> SUZANNE
> I know. Your mom called my mom. That's why I came over. I
> thought you could use someone to talk to.

> NORA JANE
> (Sitting down on her bed) I can't believe it. They never fight or...

> SUZANNE
> Well, not in front of you.

> NORA JANE
> They just walked in here and told me. I thought they were
> kidding at first.

> SUZANNE
> That would be some joke.

> NORA JANE
> They told me I could live with either one of them.

> SUZANNE
>
> Really?

 The Scene Study-guide for Young Actors!
Copyright © 2004 by Chambers Stevens

NORA JANE
Yeah.

                    SUZANNE
What are you going to do?

                    NORA JANE
I don't know. I don't know.

Fighting Words

INT. THE STAGE OF THE THEATRE

Tony is sitting on stage when Rich enters. There is a great deal of tension between them.

> RICH
>
> Hey.

> TONY
>
> What do you want?

> RICH
>
> Nothing.

> TONY
>
> Then get out of here.

> RICH
>
> Hey, it's not my fault Britney doesn't like you.

> TONY
>
> I think it is.

> RICH
>
> Well, it's not.

> TONY
>
> I think you're lying.

> RICH
>
> Look, just because she wants me instead of you doesn't mean I told her what a jerk you are.

> TONY
>
> I should just beat you up right now.

> RICH
>
> I'd like to see you try.

TONY
I'm warning you.

RICH
Tony, she doesn't like you because she doesn't like you.
I don't know what the big deal is. You didn't
even like her until last week.

TONY
The deal is you told her I was a jerk. You made her not like me.
You are the reason I'm mad.

RICH
I didn't tell her!

TONY
(Pulling a note out of his pocket) Oh, yeah? Then what's this?

Tony throws the note on the ground.

RICH
Where did you get that?

TONY
Did you write it?

A beat.

RICH
Yeah.

TONY
Then you're a liar.

RICH
I guess so.

TONY
Why?

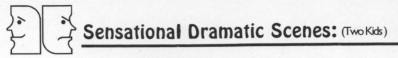

RICH
'Cause I wanted her to like me instead of you.

TONY
Well, you got what you wanted.

RICH
I guess I did.

Rich starts to walk out.

TONY
Rich.

RICH
(Turning around) Yeah?

TONY
I'm going to get you back.

RICH
I know.

TONY
You better watch out.

RICH
Don't worry, I will.

Rich exits.

 The Scene Study-guide for Young Actors!
Copyright © 2004 by Chambers Stevens

Lunch

INT. THE LUNCH ROOM

Charlie is sitting in the lunch room when Gwen walks up.

> **GWEN**
> Excuse me. I'm Gwen King. Student Council Vice President
> and Editor of the Yearbook.

> **CHARLIE**
> Yeah...?

> **GWEN**
> You're new at Andrew Jackson Middle School, aren't you?

> **CHARLIE**
> Yeah.

> **GWEN**
> Welcome. (Sitting down) Mind if I sit down? Thank you.
> Now I noticed you were sitting here in the lunchroom
> by yourself and I thought I would just...

> **CHARLIE**
> What, bug me?

> **GWEN**
> I'm sorry, I just thought...

> **CHARLIE**
> What?

> **GWEN**
> Well...that you might want to meet somebody on
> your first day here.

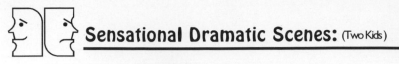

CHARLIE
If I did, it wouldn't be you.

GWEN
What is your problem?

CHARLIE
My problem? There is this girl sitting at my table bugging me.

GWEN
(Getting up) Okay, look I'm leaving. Just forget I ever said anything to you.

CHARLIE
That will be easy.

Gwen exits.

Protection

EXT. THE FRONT PORCH OF RICHARD AND MIKE'S HOUSE

Mike is sitting on the steps when Richard enters. They're both very upset.

RICHARD
There you are.

MIKE
Go away.

RICHARD
Don't be mad at me. I'm not the one who hit you.

MIKE
I didn't even do anything.

RICHARD
Yeah, I know. Once he hit me just because he said I was breathing too loud.

MIKE
Someday I'm going to hit him back! I'm going to smash...!

RICHARD
Shut up. You will not. I've got to talk to you before the police get here...

MIKE
You called the police?

RICHARD
He's been beating me for years. But when I saw him hitting you, I couldn't take it anymore.

MIKE
What will they do to him?

Copyright © 2004 by Chambers Stevens

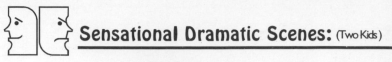

RICHARD
Arrest him. Put him in jail maybe.

MIKE
He's going to be really mad at you.

RICHARD
(Screaming) WELL I AM REALLY MAD AT HIM!

MIKE
Shut up before he comes out here.

RICHARD
I hope he rots in jail.

A beat.

MIKE
You really want him to go to jail?

RICHARD
I want him to stop drinking.

MIKE
Yeah. Me too. I'm never going to drink.

RICHARD
I'm never going to hit my kids.

MIKE
Yeah. Me either.

We start to hear the police sirens as the lights fade.

Rags

EXT. THE PORCH

Sue Bea is sitting on the porch when Chuck walks up.

> CHUCK
> My mom just told me about Rags. I'm sorry.

> SUE BEA
> Yeah...thanks.

> CHUCK
> You didn't see it happen did you?

> SUE BEA
> I saw it.

> CHUCK
> Oh.

> SUE BEA
> How many times did I tell Rags not to chase cars?

> CHUCK
> All the time. When are you going to bury him?

> SUE BEA
> My Dad's coming home right now.

> CHUCK
> (Starting to leave) Well, I'll leave you alone...

> SUE BEA
> You don't have to.

> CHUCK
> (Sitting back down) I just thought maybe you wanted
> to be by yourself.

A beat.

> SUE BEA
> I miss him already.

> CHUCK
> Remember the time Rags got chased by that skunk and...?

> SUE BEA
> (Laughing) Our house smelled for a week.

> CHUCK
> (Laughing) ...You made him a bath in tomato juice.

> SUE BEA
> I didn't want to do it.

> CHUCK
> Rags was barking the whole time.

> SUE BEA
> He hated baths.

> CHUCK
> Yeah, he did.

A beat.

> SUE BEA
> Remember that time he dug up the
> whole backyard looking for bones?

> CHUCK
> (Laughing) Your mother was so mad.

> SUE BEA
> (Joining in the laughing) She threatened to give Rags away.

CHUCK
But she didn't.

SUE BEA
No. (A beat) I kind of wish she had.

CHUCK
Why?

SUE BEA
'Cause then it wouldn't hurt so much now.

CHUCK
Yeah. I'm going to miss Rags.

SUE BEA
Me, too. He was a good friend.

CHUCK
The best.

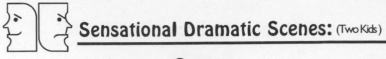

Sorry

EXT. TODD'S FRONT YARD

Todd is bouncing a ball off the side of his house. Bart enters. There is tension between them.

> BART
>
> Hey.

> TODD
>
> Hey.

> BART
>
> What are you doing?

> TODD
>
> Nothing really.

> BART
>
> Oh, okay. (He turns to leave) See you around.

> TODD
>
> What are you doing?

> BART
>
> Nothing really.

Bart starts to leave again. But then he turns around.

> BART (cont'd)
>
> I'm sorry I called you stupid.

> TODD
>
> I'm sorry I stepped on your foot.

> BART
>
> That's okay.

TODD
Does it still hurt?

                    BART
Nah. Well, maybe a little. I'm sorry I put a hole in your bike tire.

                    TODD
Well, I'm sorry I told Penny Benz you were in love with her.

                    BART
She called me three times last night.

            TODD
Sorry.

                    BART
She's actually kind of cute.

            TODD
 Penny?

                    BART
She got her braces off yesterday.

            TODD
Cool.

                    BART
(Getting up) So I guess I better go.

            TODD
Okay.

                    BART
Sorry again.

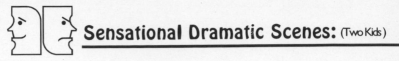

> TODD
> Yeah, me too.

Bart starts to walk off.

> TODD (cont'd)
> Hey, you want to stay and play a video game?

> BART
> If I beat you, are you going to get mad?

> TODD
> No. 'Cause you'll never beat me.

> BART
> We'll see about that. Race you to the house.

> TODD
> (Starting to run) Go!

They run off.

Twenty-One

INT. A HOSPITAL

Macy is in the hospital bed on the right. Christina is in the bed on the left.

МАСY

And that's how I broke my leg.

CHRISTINA

That is the wildest story I've ever heard.

МАСY

Yeah, it is pretty amazing. Okay, now it's your turn.
What are you in for?

CHRISTINA

Cancer.

МАСY

Oh.

CHRISTINA

They've only given me a couple of months to live.

МАСY

That's terrible.

CHRISTINA

I told the doctors I'm going to beat it. There's no way
I'm going to die so young.

МАСY

What did they say to that?

CHRISTINA

They just smiled. But I could tell they didn't believe me.
Even my mom looks at me like I'm going to die
any second.

MACY
That must be hard.

CHRISTINA
It is, kind of.

MACY
Well, I won't look at you like that.

CHRISTINA
Thanks.

MACY
In fact, I'll make a deal with you. When we grow up, say when we turn twenty-one, I'll call you and we'll do something together.

CHRISTINA
Like what?

MACY
I don't know. Is there anything you've always wanted to do?

CHRISTINA
Yeah! Jump out of an airplane!

MACY
With a parachute?

CHRISTINA
Of course, silly.

MACY
Good. I don't want to break my other leg.

CHRISTINA
(Laughing) You've got yourself a deal. When we turn twenty-one, we'll go parachuting together.

MACY

Cool.

A beat.

CHRISTINA

(This is hard for her to say) Thanks for believing in me.

MACY

(Trying not to cry) Don't worry about it.
You're going to be okay.

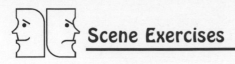
Sensational

Scene Exercises

for Kids!

Here are a few fun exercises to do with the scenes you just read.

1. Play THE OPPOSITE

Many young actors read the script and immediately decide how to play the scene. For example, if the character says she's a ballerina, then the actress will stand on her toes. For an acting exercise, *play the opposite*. Suppose that one of the characters is a football player. Why not have him move like a ballerina? Or the ballerina move like a football player. This works especially well in comedy.

2. PICK AN ACTION

Young actors working on scenes often do nothing but say their lines. Both actors look each other in the eye and talk. But in real life, we rarely just stare at each other and talk. Most of us do two things at once. Take a quick look at the scene called *Fighting Words*. The two characters in this scene are in an argument. Even though the scene is short, it will be boring if all the actors do is stand and yell at each other. Try picking an action to get you moving. Have both performers fishing, baiting their hooks, casting their fishing lines, or maybe even nabbing a big one. Try all different kinds of actions with each scene. You will be surprised how much better your acting will be.

3. FINISH THE SCENE

You have probably noticed that many of the scenes do not have an ending. Take the scene *Excuses*. Bonnie has

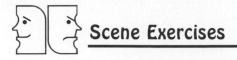

Scene Exercises

caught Lee in a lie. Once she catches her hat, what does she do? We don't know because this is where the scene stops. Well, try finishing the scene. Maybe Bonnie makes Lee help her decorate. Maybe Lee runs. You don't need to write these various endings on paper. Improvise. Play around with many different endings.

4. IMPROVISE WITH THE CHARACTER'S HISTORY

Let's take the scene *Space School*. Wiget is trying to teach Ivory how to fly. Why not make up a scene where Wiget is being built? Or maybe a scene where Ivory teaches Wiget how to dance? The more you improvise with the characters, the more you know about them.

5. GIBBERISH

This is one of my favorite exercises. Gibberish is a sound that cannot be understood. Like blah blah blah blah. To the audience, it looks like the actor is speaking a foreign language. Try the scenes using Gibberish. This is a good exercise for an actor who is acting his lines like he is a robot. Gibberish breaks that pattern and helps the actor find a whole new meaning to the scene.

Try all of these exercises. And remember, have fun with them.

Glossary of Industry Terms

Show business has its own interesting vocabulary. The word *wings*, for example. When someone tells you to go *stand in the wings*, they mean stand on the *side of the stage*, not on the wings of a bird. I asked a number of the kids I coach to tell me their definitions for some of these important theater/film words. Sometimes kids can explain things more clearly than adults.

AD LIB - To make up words not already in the script. If a director tells you to ad lib, what he means is ignore the script and say something your character would say.

AFTRA - Stands for the "American Federation of Television and Radio Artists.". AFTRA is a union for actors.

AGENT - A person who helps you get acting jobs. And then takes 10% of your earnings.

AIR DATE - The date that your commercial shows on TV.

ATMOSPHERE - See "Extra."

AUDITION - The show biz word for "trying out" for a commercial.

BEAT - A moment. If the script says, "A beat," then that means take a small pause before you say your next line.

BLOCKING - Stage Movement. When the director gives you blocking he is telling you where to stand and when to move.

BOOK - When you "book" a commercial that means that you have "won" the audition.

BOOM - A microphone that is held above your head.

BREAK-A-LEG - An actor's way of saying "Good Luck."

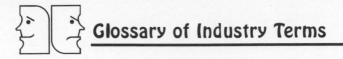

Glossary of Industry Terms

CALLBACK - The second audition.

CASTING DIRECTOR - The person hired by the producer to find the right actors for the job.

CATTLE CALL - See "Open Call."

CENTER STAGE - Right in the middle of the stage. (see diagram on page 102)

CLIENT - The person who has final say on a commercial. If it is a Pepsi commercial then Pepsi is the client.

CUE - Any signal that it is your turn to speak or move. If the director says "pick up your cues," he means that when the other actor stops talking, you must start quicker.

CUE CARD - A piece of poster board with the actor's lines on it.

DIALOGUE - The lines you speak from your script.

DIRECTOR - The person who is in charge of the play or film. He or she instructs the actors, set designers, and every other part of the play or film.

DOWNSTAGE - The front of the stage closest to the audience. The opposite of Upstage. (see diagram on page 104)

EXTRA - A nonspeaking part. An extra appears in the background of the scene. Also called Atmosphere.

FOCUS - Putting all your attention on one thing. If a director yells "focus," he/she means "Listen up."

GESTURE - The way you move your arms and hands.

HAND PROPS - Small things used by the actor. Like a purse or a baseball.

Glossary of Industry Terms

HEADSHOT - An 8" X 10" black and white picture of an actor.

IMPROVISATION - Acting without a script. Making it up as you go along.

LINES - The words you speak from the script. Learning your lines means to memorize the speeches your character has in the script.

OFFSTAGE - The parts of the stage the audience can't see.

OPEN CALL - An audition where you don't need an appointment. Also called a *Cattle-call* because open calls usually have tons of people.

OSCAR - An annual award given by The Academy of Motion Pictures, Arts and Sciences. There are Oscars awarded for all aspects of film work, including acting, directing, and screen-writing.

PRINCIPAL - The main acting role in a commercial.

PULITZER PRIZE - An annual writing award established in 1917. The award is given by the Pulitzer board made up of newspaper editors, writers, and professors of major universities.

RESIDUAL - Money paid to an actor for the repeat showing of a commercial or TV show.

SAG - Stands for "Screen Actors Guild." SAG is a union for actors.

SIDES - Part of a script. When you audition, they give you sides to read from.

SLATE - What the casting director says at the beginning of a commercial audition. It means say your name and what agency represents you.

STAGE LEFT - When you are standing center stage facing the audience, stage left is to your left. (see diagram on page 102)

STAGE RIGHT - When you are standing center stage facing the audience, stage right is to your right. (see diagram on page 102)

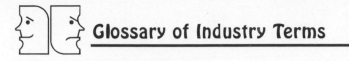

Glossary of Industry Terms

STAND-IN - Extras who "stand-in" for the lead actors while the crew focuses lights.

TONY AWARD - An annual award given by the American Theatre Wing. The award was established in 1947. To qualify for a Tony Award, the play or musical must have been performed on Broadway. The Tony is awarded for all aspects of theatre work, including acting, directing, and set design.

TOP - The beginning. When the director says, "Go from the top," he or she means start at the beginning.

UPGRADE - Being "upgraded" means when you are hired as an extra and the director gives you a line or makes you a principal.

UPSTAGE - The back of the stage. The opposite of Downstage. (see diagram below)

WINGS - The sides of a stage. If the actor stands in the wings, he or she is not seen. (see diagram below)

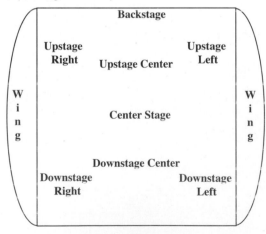

Bibliography: Sensational Films With Young Actors

I get asked all the time, what are my favorite movies starring kids? Well, you asked and here they are, in no particular order. I highly recommend that you watch your favorite movies, and mine, keeping an eye on how these young actors do what they do so well. Hey, homework that's educational and fun! What more could you ask for?

<u>E.T. The Extra-Terrestrial</u> One of the most popular films of all time. Henry Thomas and Drew Barrymore are great as the kids who rescue E.T.; Directed by Steven Speilberg (PG)

<u>Mary Poppins</u> A great musical. Julie Andrews is fantastic as the nanny who can do anything. (G)

<u>Willy Wonka and the Chocolate Factory</u> The wonderful story of a boy, Charlie, who inherits a chocolate factory. (G)

<u>My Dog Skip</u> Frankie Muniz from <u>Malcolm in the Middle</u> has a lot of fun as the boy who gets his first dog named Skip. (PG)

<u>The Secret of Roan Irish</u> A magical movie about a young girl who goes to live with her grandparents in a small fishing village in Ireland. (PG)

<u>A Little Princess</u> The ultimate girl's movie. A young girl is sent to a boarding school when her father is presumed dead. (G)

<u>Oliver!</u> A musical about a group of pickpockets. The songs are fun and Jack Wild is great as "The Artful Dodger." (Not rated).

<u>Miracle on 34th Street</u> A great Christmas film about a girl who doesn't believe in Santa Claus. Natalie Wood is spectacular. (Not Rated)

Bibliography: Sensational Films
With Young Actors

<u>Home Alone</u> The ultimate boy's film. Macaulay Culkin rocks as the boy who is left home alone. (PG)

<u>Old Yeller</u> One of the saddest films ever made. Another boy-and-his-dog film. Guaranteed to break your heart.

<u>Goonies</u> This film is a blast from start to finish. A group of kids stumble upon a treasure map and outwit a group of thieves.

<u>Matilda</u> Sara Wilson is hilarious as Matilda, the girl with telekinetic powers.

<u>Escape to Witch Mountain</u> An awesome tale about a couple of kids with telepathic powers. The sequel, <u>Return to Witch Mountain</u> is fun, too.

<u>Freaky Friday</u> A mother and daughter magically switch bodies. Disney does it again.

<u>Bedknobs and Broomsticks</u> A fun musical about a bed that flies.

<u>Bad News Bears</u> They can't play baseball. Their coach can't coach. And yet, when the going gets tough, they win.

<u>Swiss Family Robinson</u> Every kids' dream. Stranded on a desert island. Fighting pirates. Skipping school.

<u>Chitty Chitty Bang Bang</u> The best flying car film ever made. And once you see the movie, you won't be able to get the title song out of your head.

<u>The Sixth Sense</u> Haley Joel Osmont's performance is guaranteed to give you nightmares. Watch out. (PG-13)

Index